When & If

New Poems

When & If

New Poems by

DeWitt Clinton

© 2025 DeWitt Clinton. All rights reserved.
This material may not be reproduced in any form, published,
reprinted, recorded, performed, broadcast,
rewritten or redistributed without
the explicit permission of DeWitt Clinton.
All such actions are strictly prohibited by law.

Cover design by Shay Culligan
Cover image by Jeanie Tomasko
Author photo by Moroccan camel driver

ISBN: 978-1-63980-786-4
Library of Congress Control Number: 2025943310

Kelsay Books
502 South 1040 East, A-119
American Fork, Utah 84003
Kelsaybooks.com

Acknowledgments

Grateful acknowledgment is made to the editors of the following periodicals in which these poems previously appeared:

A Plate of Pandemic: "When & If"
Across the Margin: "Deep Deep Space," "The Plan," "Then Nothing"
American Writers Review: "Blue Hands Blue Fingers," Turmoil and Recovery issue
Anti-Heroin Chic: "What Did You Just Say?" "Right as Rain"
Arts + Literature Lab: "After Rumi's 'The Guest House'"
The Bezine: "So Enticing, So Delectable, So Now," "Oh Nothing Much, You?" "Anytime, Possibly," "Somehow, Soon, We'll Ascend into the Clouds"
Deronda Review {Israel}: "After "Insomnia"
Live Encounters: "Anybody Home?" "A Few Chickadees Alight in the Dying Lilacs," "Just Not Yet," "On Reading Luminous Poems in an Escape While Outside, Corona Drops People Off at the Curb, Or at the Nearby Hospital, Or Morgue," "Not Generalizable, But That Doesn't Matter, Does It?" "Joy of Wine," Who Wants That?" "Knock, Knock, Who's There?"
Lothlorien Poetry Journal: "A Simple Zero-Sum Conundrum," "On Fire," "Troubled," "Yes, Dear, Only I Didn't Say Yes, Dear"
Love in the Time of Covid {New Zealand}: "That Lovely Evening in Lublin," "Dusted"
Misfit Magazine: "After Reading Yehuda Amichai's 'The School Where I Studied,' I Do Wonder What I've Learned After So Many Lessons, Lectures," "O Soothest Sleep"
Muddy River Poetry Review: "Who Isn't Thinking Like That, Like You?" "Goodnight All, Sweet Dreamy Dreams"

New Verse News: "As Time Goes By," "Did You See "Groundhog Day" the Other Night?" "Now the Dying Who Are Almost Dead, Are Dead"
One Art Poetry: "Sitting Shiva," "Burial at Sea"
The Writing Disorder: "Not Exactly," "So So, So Let's Order Carry Out," "Then There's That"
Verse-Virtual: "Hang in There," "If Not Now, When?" "O Beatrice," "An Elucidation on Death and Dying"

Also by DeWitt Clinton

Full-Length Collections

Hello There
By a Lake Near a Moon: Fishing with the Chinese Masters
At the End of the War
The Coyot. Inca Texts
The Conquistador Dog Texts

Chapbooks

Active Death: Unholy Rhymes
Furnace: A Ballet Performance
Night Jungle Bird Life
das Illustrite Mississippithal Revisited
Wrong Continent: Stories of Travel
The Rand McNally Poems

Edited and Co-Edited Journals

Sofer: A Publication of the Jewish Writer's Workshop (Olin Sang Ruby Union Institute)
Eleven Wisconsin Poets (Vol. I, Vol. II)
An Americas Anthology: A Geopoetics Landmark
Salthouse: A Geopoetics Journal

Contents

I: Somehow, Soon, We'll Ascend into the Clouds

So Enticing, So Delectable, So Now	19
Blue Hands Blue Fingers	21
That Lovely Evening in Lublin	22
Dusted	25
Did You See "Groundhog Day" the Other Night?	27
On Reading Luminous Poems in an Escape, While Outside, Corona Drops People Off at the Curb, Or at the Nearby Hospital, Or Morgue	29
After Rumi's "The Guest House"	30
Not Exactly	31
Oh, Nothing Much, You?	33
Who Wants That?	35
I'm Sorry, What Was That?	37
After Reading Yehuda Amichai's "The School Where I Studied," I Do Wonder What I've Learned After So Many Lessons, Lectures	39
Anytime, Possibly	41
Somehow, Soon, We'll Ascend into the Clouds	43

II: A Few Chickadees Alight in the Dying Light

Anybody Home?	47
What Did You Just Say?	48
So, We're All Going to Die, Right?	50
Now the Dying Who Are Almost Dead, Are Dead	52
A Few Chickadees Alight in the Dying Lilacs	54
When & If	56
O soothest Sleep! if so it please thee, close in midst of this thine hymn my willing eyes	58
Not Generalizable, But That Doesn't Matter, Does It?	60

Just Not Yet	61
Then, There's That	62
Deep Deep Space	63
As Time Goes By	65
"... if not now, when?"	66
O Beatrice	67
Right as Rain	68

III: Sitting Shiva

Hang in There	73
Sitting Shiva	75
Then, Nothing	76
The Plan	77
Yes, Dear, Only I Didn't Say Yes, Dear	78
It's Time, My Dear	79
Knock Knock, Who's There?	80
Who Isn't Thinking Like That, Like You?	81
So	85
On Fire	86
After "Insomnia"	87
Troubled	89
So So, So Let's Order Carry-Out	91
A Simple Zero-Sum Conundrum	92
Reading "Joy of Wine," With Li Ch'ing-Chao to the Tune of "A Dream Song," Many Centuries Later, Near a Great Lake	94
Goodnight All, Sweet Dreamy Dreams	95
An Elucidation on Death and Dying	96
Burial at Sea	98
Wouldn't That Be Something?	99

Preface to When & If

This collection is as much a fugue, a sustained elegy, or Kaddish, as well as a sobering eulogy as so many of our dear friends and those we've never ever known around the world, are now not here on Earth, so how can we possibly understand what happened in this terribly long pandemic? Perhaps these poems will help us to reflect on what just happened, globally, and in our homes as well.

This collection has few, if any, stanza breaks as somehow, these poems are more of a complaint without the artifice of art. Perhaps some will read these laments as a therapeutic response to all we've experienced, but please know writing these poems has helped immensely, all written in the hopes they might offer solace and comfort to all from this long night.

DeWitt Clinton
The Village of Shorewood, Wisconsin

I:
Somehow, Soon,
We'll Ascend into the Clouds

So Enticing, So Delectable, So Now

Just think about it please, and don't worry a bit
as no one lasts that long anyway, but here's what's
what. I am still here, and so glad to know you
are still here, but then, what can we make of
all those who now are not here, and somehow
I'd like to be acquainted with all those who have
up and left us, in spite of all the care and love
everyone hoped who could save you, and all those
who probably inhaled the wrong wisp of air
that promised an early death to you and all
those close to you, and this is what we all
wonder about, as we try to go about wondering
how in the heck did any of us every plan for
something as wicked and invasive as something
like this, and nobody, nobody ever wants this
to keep dropping people, some of whom are
as close to us as a wife, or a loved one, or our
dear grandparents who we love so much, but
are now gasping for air, and wondering who
just now breathed this deadly gasp of air
which now has infected almost all of us who
seem to not have any idea that we're
on the way out, even though most of us
had hoped for a lovely evening with all
of us gathered around a plate of such
delectables what we all so wanted to
taste and savor and toast to our beautiful
loved ones who we simply cannot imagine
not being here tomorrow as we're now
at the crematorium, wondering why Julie
and Maurice are now measuring just how
high the temperature is to send all of us who

know how flesh will slowly sear to invisibility
into what's left of ash and bone, and possibly
we'll be there too, in just a few days, as
nobody really knows who's coughed and
sprayed so many unknown travelers that
sooner or later, as in, pretty soon, you and
perhaps even me, well, we're all going to
end up as ash and bone, and nobody will
ever remember any of this in even a few
years, but isn't this what everybody predicted,
that sooner or later, all of us would inhale
someone else, and then we'd be the un-
fortunate one who stopped breathing
in only a few minutes, and no one no one
knew exactly what had just happened
even though no one no one really expected
something like this, for even the neighbors
asked, are you okay, and of course, no one could
even wonder that no one no one was okay as all
of us, or most of us, will leave the earth for ever
and no one no one wanted any of this to happen
except for a small harmless creature as so few
knew anything about what was harvested for its
flesh, and then, quite surprisingly, we all just died
just like that, sometimes in a matter of just
a few minutes, and how, how could that
be something we thought was so cute, so
charming, so delectable, so enticing, so now?

Blue Hands Blue Fingers

These blue hands, slightly sticky, slightly smooth,
almost wet the longer one chooses what to wear,
keeping all of us one fabric from soon being taken
to a ventilator so the lungs can do what the lungs
cannot do, breathe for us when we find no way
of breathing on our own, these blue fingers, these
masks which prevent what might filter into our
lungs which we so often assumed would keep us
breathing along for ages, or years, or months, but
now just a few more days if that's even possible,
all of us under containment, under isolation, all
due to a pangolin, taken as a rare delicacy by a
few who regard this the tastiest of meats one
can savor, but the bat droppings the old ancestor
ate were alive with viruses none of us had ever
ever heard of and so many confused it with a
delicious beer that so many confused the beer
with the pangolin, though it was much too late
as those who had already fallen in streets all
throughout the world had now become what so
many feared that a virus had set out to take out
so many of us, all at once, and no one, no one
knew exactly what had happened to so many
all at once, as if a meteor flew in unannounced
and now the clouds above us, the air inside us
was what all of us could not understand as all
of us didn't even have time to prepare papers
for anyone who might have survived, lived to
say this is what happened, as none of us want
what happened to happen to us, not now, ever.

That Lovely Evening in Lublin

You've thought this too, right, that you're trying
to remember what happened just the other day,
or perhaps something so far back it's now hard
to even try to reconstruct, but isn't that the way
an old mind can only live with so much stuff,
that some of it just has to be tossed, but when
exactly did we lose all those precious memories
that make up some of who we were and thought
we'd remember forever, but even without our
permission, some of it just gets thrown out,
tossed, but when and how is so unclear and no
one really keeps records of what's about to
take leave, as the brain is shrinking, right, about
this time, even my brother can't remember the
two of us, mowing around old gravestones,
but those stones look so much tidier,
as if anybody down there really cared as
even the families are probably all gone by
now, but then one day we're stuck on a bit
of a memory of that last picnic on the
(forgot the name) river, and nothing seems
to loosen up in the old brain not even what
we ate, or drank, or said, or felt, and what's
so odd about all this is that all of us enjoyed
those lovely moments, listening, laughing,
lifting another one, and another part of me
might have been taking notes getting the
quotes just right, and then, where the heck
did it go, as if it's just something someone
somewhere decided to delete just like that
as the roof in our head just couldn't take
anymore without crashing into what's

below, and what's below has hardly any
way of knowing what we did on that lovely
summer evening on the river bank we'd
never been to, but was so delicious for
both of us, especially when we just wandered
away from the fire and then found ourselves
wrapped around each other even though
we'd just found each other a few days
before, or was it a week or a month before
when I walked into the party you were hosting
or was it your husband, the one you'll never
see again, and now, unfolding all those
years so long ago that sometimes I wonder if
all the drama stored up there has its own
stage, with props and costumes, even lights,
it must, or how could any of these scenes
ever get passed even the opening lines, but
now, nobody, nobody can't even recall
who walks on first to open the first lines,
and worse, no one, ever, is sitting out
there as there's barely enough room
for all the make-shift stages, and costume
changes especially when the mind drifts
from one drama to another without even
knowing we're someplace else, so all the
loving pets, all the belts released for
thrashing all the little ones, all the clothes
that no longer fit, all the delightful ideas
lost before even remembering, all the
songs hummed, or sung as if we were
still at the opera in Lublin, all lost, even
the potato soup across from the opera

house, as rain poured and poured on the
cobblestones outside making what we
thought was the most memorable ever
evening, now slipping away, the rain,
the opera of Verdi's so stunning especially
in this old city of war, now mostly forgotten
by all the young, as something is always
moving into the space, something forgotten
always lost, tossed, turning into fragments,
then nothing, except maybe here when
we try to put together what we knew about
that evening, Verdi's opera about all those
Israelites marching into exile, the pretend
moment we saw Bogart and Bergmann
walking by, arm in arm, looking in to see
the two of us, looking up, somewhat surprised,
on that evening we loved so much in Lublin.

Dusted

I'm quite lost, though I don't know what just
happened where something I once knew about
suddenly is missing, as in I placed something
somewhere, though someone whispered just
the other day that it has now turned first to
wood from an old redwood, and now it's almost
petrified. Of course, this is a mystery to everyone,
including you of course, as you will probably
pretend you know nothing about what is now
so lost, no one can even remember what it was
once before, when it was not lost, but that's
not quite the point, is it, so we're here, trying
to figure out if someone has pulled a hood
over everything that was once beautiful, and
now whenever we can even glance at it, all
we see is a faded mirror of what it once was,
but really, what was it the first place that
was so precious, so tender, so passionate
that none of us could even get any sleep
as we were so consumed by what that was,
but the mystery, for both of us, is not so
much where it is now, but tell me, just
how do you think all of this misery surprised
us as if we just awoke on the bed we slept
in forever, and now, even when we shake
the blankets just a little to make up what
we thought was ours, all we have is a tiny
dust storm of flying motes and possibly in-
flight creatures so disturbed by what once
was, but that's what it must be, don't you
think, weren't you here that evening when
all just began to float away without any

sense of what made any of it lift into the
night air like that, that by the next morning
no one no one knows how to talk about
what happened, and before, everyone was
so pleasant, so conversational, so loving, and
now we can't even figure out where everyone
has gone, as if something tiny entered into
all our loved ones, and without even a hacking
cough, or a chest so tight, or a fever that
makes us chip our teeth, suddenly, we have
just disappeared like that, and no one wants
to even get close to what is now a corpse
which just minutes before was someone
we loved so much, but then, perhaps it really
is as someone just asked, is this the end?
And why didn't anyone know that, now that
we're gone, not here, dusted, quite lost.

Did You See "Groundhog Day" the Other Night?

Too many days identical to identical days though
identical days are far better than having no identical
days left, as in that was the last identical day we spent
but then, you'll be coming along soon I suspect, just
as the rest of us don't really have a lifetime left though
everyone is saying we'll get over this, through this, we'll
make it, just take big deep breaths, eat Brussel sprouts,
ease up on the whites and reds or for our friend up the
road, the foreign sounding frothy drink he ends each day
with, but really, it's only not so bad if someone you know
doesn't call or send a text or drop in on a video check
as the bad boy virus is going to take way too many of us
even if we keep a positive glow about all that's happened
so far, and the reports of available masks made across
the oceans, the make-shift ventilators, the gloves that
seem to tear even as we put them on, perhaps it'll just
be that unmasked ungloved shopper eager to stock up
on a basket of groceries, Charmin, Bounty, Clorox wipes,
or just about anything that might convince us we're clean,
we're not sick, we don't have a dry cough just a cough
now and then, and our temp is about the same as it's
always been, and the chest occasionally feels all wound
up, but it's probably just something we ate that gives
us such a burn that would put any of us into a panic
over is this it, is this what we're trying to dodge, is this
tasty tiny bat going to take us all out, like this, right now?
Well, yes, as the bad bug seems to constantly evolve
into something we can't even begin to imagine, though
whatever it is, we're just never going to know exactly
how to take the bugger out, just like granny did years
ago when she twirled that chicken around and around
then placed the goofy neck out nice and straight so

no one would have to wonder, ever again, what some
of us, but not all of us, might be salivating again as
by sundown, the table is set, parts are frying, and
we just hope everybody we knew yesterday will
be knocking on the door, hoping there's still a chance
that tomorrow will be another chance for another
identical day that will help us to get through what
some of us actually look forward to, something totally
identical.

On Reading Luminous Poems in an Escape, While Outside, Corona Drops People Off at the Curb, Or at the Nearby Hospital, Or Morgue

If it helps, the time is early afternoon, sheltered in a covered
parking lot waiting for someone to draw a blood sample
of someone else. The wind outside makes everything
move in a way that something natural is about to happen.
Most but not all are masked. The storm is coming soon.
Everything will be soaked. We have two more weeks,
or months, or more, of lockdown. The virus may never
leave. One by one, it will find us, on every continent.
In a few minutes we will make lunch, find a movie set
in deep space, where we cannot go or even visit but we
decide to go anyway. Each time when we go out, if we
go out again, we will measure two weeks before either
or both of us falls down and dies. If we don't fall down,
we think we can outlive what's out there, but a dear friend
tells us just wait, try to pretend what could never end,
and that's just what we're going to do, right after lunch.

After Rumi's "The Guest House"

—This being human is a guest house.

Go right ahead, invite the uninvited
guest even if the guest will stay too
long, ravish all that's in your house
even those who come to mourn not
knowing how long the visit will last,
and most unexpectedly, will probably
follow everyone out, and you, when
everybody's skin and bones, and then
bones, and then dust into the wind.
The guest doesn't really care a bit
who you are, only that you're there,
or here, for that matter, and no
brooms, no vacuums, no, nothing
will do you any good so be nice,
say hello, don't even ask how long
the guest wants to stay, maybe even
make some drinks if you're still able,
or if not, say something smart, even
if what you say won't matter a bit.

Not Exactly

We're here, just like you thought we were here,
but not for long, so don't get your hopes up,
at least not that much as who knows what
might happen even before we get to the end.
Isn't that what you've heard somewhere,
that even though you're certainly having one
hell of a time, it will soon fade, and then, very
likely, you might not even remember who
was where, at least I can't, and please say
exactly why you can remember everyone
you've ever kissed, or smooched a bit with or
held a hand, heck, it's hard just to remember
anything yesterday, let alone all the times
we've been in contact with someone else
out there, so just don't try to make a big
deal out of it, and enjoy what you have
right now, because believe me, and I'm
not the only one who knows this, it's
more than likely not going to turn out
like you hoped it would, and why should
it, after all, that would be something like
listening to the same old 45 over and over
and who has 45's anyway, so please don't
open up that old closet of yours and
pull down or sort through all of those
albums you've collected and not listened
to for years, and remember, every single
one of them is going to sound a bit scratchy,
and will probably disappoint something
huge, but that's what's going to happen
if you keep going back through all your
stuff like that, so just call up the haul

away, your old memories guy, as he'll
make more money on what you've
forgotten than you could ever believe,
really, so what's wrong with that,
and he'll play them once or twice,
nodding and maybe even boogying
down a bit like he used to, but then
he'll sell them to a dealer, and then
they'll just collect dust until some
old fan will finger her way through
what was yours, and then, well, sheer
delight for her, and you, sadly will
not be in the mood for any music,
no sir, as you'll be out of here, no
memories whatsoever, as you're not
here now, even though you pretended
that you'd be here on an unlimited
visit, but that's the problem, isn't
it, we just don't know what's next
do we, even though we saunter a
bit thinking this is it, something we
all want to savor, so go ahead savor,
but somewhere in that poor brainpan
of yours, remember, you're already
gone.

Oh, Nothing Much, You?

Well, yes, we do have a few puny, pale yellow day lilies
bursting forth in our little universe, the size of the lot
I'd have to look up if you're that curious, and I've set
down some tiny grass seeds near the sidewalk to
replace whacked grass the mowing crew always likes
to take down to the nub. Other than that, we're looking
forward to more movies which we've already seen,
and we're always tempted to see "Burn After Reading"
again, and maybe again, as it's fun to say the lines along
with the hilarious discombobulated, but we know none
of it's true, but we always think it is, and it is, of course,
somewhere, but not here, yet, though the way things
are developing around here, anything might pop in
into our tiny little universe. Of course, we're gloved
and masked, as we have no way to know where those
tiny floating bugs are that want to slip down our nose
into our old lungs, and since both of them, hers and
mine, are not exactly in great shape, we're doing all
we know how to do, but we do get very frightened
nearly all the time, always, so we turn on the telly
and learn that we're back to April with even higher
infections so that makes both of us want to stop
breathing at all, but then, after a few seconds we
gasp for air, having no real assurances from anyone
we're not already lined up to be stacked in the morgue
like so many of our dear friends have ended up, but
if you think about it, and haven't you had time to
think about it as well, well, we're mostly into survival
mode, eating more asparagus and Brussels sprouts
that we would never have dreamed of but we're
hopeful the sandstorm from the Sahara will not only

blot out all the light around here, but also give a
good whack to those floating, nasty critters who
don't like at all a sandblasting into their micro—
impossible-to-believe-they're-still-here-with-us.
Yes, pour some more of that, and how's-by-you?

Who Wants That?

It could be worse, of course, but who wants what
is already really bad to get worse, as in, Holy Cow
Worse, as in, that's bad, or very bad or some kind
of Bad Bad that only the worst are boo-hooing
about right now, as this is something that brings
out the best or worst of those who skipped out
after third grade thinking nothing more needed
up there, except something is needed up there,
but not what's there now, no, not ever needed
though it's going to be a tough go to try to even
speak evenhandedly but if we even used that
word once, we'd probably be on the ground
with a terrible amount of blood staining what
was once a decent sidewalk only now it's more
like a hardpan gurney with a bloody head, bruised
ribs, swollen lips, and leaky eyes, so who wants
that, really, so there's going to always be that
quick hesitation before going in and saying Stop
What You Are Doing, but before we even get the
command from outer open space, when BAM we're
down and out on the gurney, and what, whatever
made us think we could talk our way out of or into
this mess some call a mess and others just think
of it as just as a cool *brouhaha* as there's not much
else to do as we all get closer and closer to the edge
of space where somebody, somebody is yelling from
somewhere Stop Doing That, and those doing just
that start the old belly jelly roll just before the bat
comes out to rearrange whatever thoughts we once
had up there about fair and square, so here comes
the first pitch, and we duck a bit too slowly, and try
to stand up straight as the second windup is out

there, spinning, aiming for a better contact between
bat and head, and it's a hit, a bloody hit, and then
we're down, face down, with a steel toe kicking
in the old kidney and we're wondering that maybe
it's really going to be worse, but then, it will be
worse, and who out there, who, who wants that?

I'm Sorry, What Was That?

It's bad enough, but getting worse as more and more of us
can't even remember what we did just yesterday, which
was quite special, but now, no one has a clue as to why.
So this is where it ends, I'm told, all those memories and
delights stored away until something triggers it loose for
a he-haw, or a deep sigh, or just dreaming back to when
it was, but it's looking like it wasn't was, and that's getting
harder and harder to take, especially when your own kin
can't recall whether or not he has a sister, or what did
you do yesterday? You're pretty clear on that, aren't you?
But to be honest, we're lucky that we're still here, licking
ice cream cones, or for the lucky ones, spooning up treats
out of a bowl. Luckily no one in our block is slobbering,
but then, we're all tucked into our houses for the next
decade, aren't we, due to billions of bugs which no one
can see or hear or feel or touch, until, of course, they
land and stay too long in our old lungs, and no matter
how we're turned, or asked to cough, or perhaps the
lovely dinner doesn't ever again waft into the olfactory
nodes as even that's gone, and if that isn't enough,
more and more of us are saying, What's That? as if
what we just said went in on the left side and slid
right out of the right as if nothing happened but that's
happened to you, hasn't it? But if you're lucky and say
no to all of this, just wait, the lovely life we've lived,
or not, is not going to continue on lovely paths of flowers
and fir trees. No, it's going to end up with more and more
wild beasts residing in our brains scarring the be-Jesus
out of us, and of course, our loved ones who have just
about lost their patience, and a good walk out the door
just doesn't seem to help as it did a few years ago.
Frankly, and I'll admit this isn't very well thought out,

I'd just as soon sign up indefinitely for a cruise knowing
those bugs are probably floating above everyone standing
too close in line for the buffet lunch, but perhaps if we
can plan to spend all of our day out on the decks breathing
in that cold ocean air, wherever it is, then maybe we've
got a chance to deboard one gigantic cruiser and taxi over
to the next one which will take us out further and further.
These behemoths haven't reported any major sinkings, but
that doesn't sound quite so bad if one can just get to the life
rafts as all of us have to practice rafting even before first night's
dinner with everyone, guests and crew, all milling around with
the finest trays of delights, but then, someone said we don't
get to choose how we go, but from where we are now, it seems
so much more reasonable than laying out in a white sheet bed
with nurses arriving with huge frowns knowing we've done
the no-no again, and then somebody has to wipe up all the stink,
until it happens all over again, so for heaven's sake, please stop
with those polite smiles, and thoughtful nods, and let's all find
something that will take all of this away, into something none
of us knows anything about, but if that bothers a few, well,
who's up for a round or two of parcheesi, yes?

After Reading Yehuda Amichai's "The School Where I Studied," I Do Wonder What I've Learned After So Many Lessons, Lectures

The places of my old school desks, some
with flip tops, some with tables that just
lifted you up and out, well, I can't find
any of them now, but I'm still studying,
always hungry for why is that or who
thinks that about that. I've learned a
few things, but most of what I've learned
I've forgotten, and don't want to even
try to get back to those long lessons.
The sciences were always way too
much to absorb the way we had to
absorb so much so quickly. I may have
even failed astronomy, and I'm still
wondering about the names of weeds
that still appear unexpectedly in the
back yard, unwanted, even bitter they're
there. Now I'm a big history buff, and
don't mind at all reading about civilizations
that hadn't even become civilizations just
yet. Of course, I forget quickly all that
happened, then. The windows of the
house where I live in now are closed
to keep out all the bugs and weeds,
though I don't look up too often when
studying something new, as I'm probably
there, briefly, and not here, wondering
what chore I have to do right away.
Ask some of my friends, but I wasn't
a big playground player, though I did

like to spin and spin on the merry-go-round.
Sadly, I haven't met anyone I wanted
to love even close to a school yard,
but that's not so important now, is it?
Still, I wouldn't miss walking through
a museum over and over, even if I
was there before, sometime, the joy
of reading little stories behind glass
or plexiglass is just about all that
I can remember, for now, about then.

Anytime, Possibly

Someday, one of us isn't going to be around
the other, and that hasn't happened before,
except for the occasional trip to you know where,
or other times which are now so hard to put
back into our old brains now, but then,
each one of us wants the other to step up
to what each of us can't imagine, and lately
I've seen a lot of old friends do the very same
thing, step up, cope, figure it out, go out
for a walk, maybe all day, though then there'd
be less food on our little bed trays, and of
course, less trash, overall, but one of those
days, we'd start to wonder how we're going
(and it's not exactly we're going) to cope with
all those dresses and suits and shoes downstairs
which one of us said, let someone else take
care of that, and I think I know who that's
going to be, so I'll step up, or down, and see
what's there that's going to different stores
that might want to feature all the fashions
one of us is no longer wearing and just the
thought of that makes me think I'll wear black
or white all day, maybe all night, yet for what
reason I have no idea, though I sense a lot
of single spouses might wonder the same thing,
getting used to not saying, "I'm home," when
of course, you're home, not you, but me, of
course there's the cat, so the "I'm home"
could be just as good as before, but not before
pets to the head, or tail, hearing a little squeak
which for the present, will have to do. That
seems about right doesn't it, the sort of that

will have to do, at least for a while, until
something else unexpected might go wrong,
and then someone else will have to finish
what I couldn't get around to with all that time.

Somehow, Soon, We'll Ascend into the Clouds

Thanks for even wondering if we're still here as
we don't step out that much anymore, and our
last dining out ended up carrying it all back home,
but it was tasty, especially the grilled tuna with
all those delicious peppers and onions nestled
nicely together in warm cubed feta and olives
which makes all of us wish we were back again
on the Mediterranean island where we took
a lift straight up the mountain side to behold
island top shops and restaurants just for the
curious who were living off shore in spacious
apartments, some with balconies, so we could
all gaze out over the blue waters to watch dolphins
sail so happily just above the waves, but that
was long ago, wasn't it, and now we're in lock-
down hoping to save our old lungs from what
none of us ever expected to travel around the
globe with such frightening speed, as if one war
wasn't enough, a plague-like flu wiped away
so many who had just entered into the new
and frightening world which some of us
can still remember, not the first part, as that
would make us older than anything living
on the planet, and so much is no longer
living, but we are hopeful, as just yesterday
astronomers applauded the possibility of life
on Venus, though getting there, from here,
seems a long shot, and possibly not in our
lifetime, but that's really beside the point,
isn't it, as all we really have is the idea that
clouds out there, somewhere, might drift
toward earth in several million years, long
after Aunt Lucy or cousin Geraldine have

turned to dust as by then almost everything
will be dust, and that's what we really wonder
about after all this effort, to find something,
something interesting, only to know by then
the planet will probably recreate itself and
to our delight, a few will crawl out of the
cesspool oceans, and make a life on a beach,
something like the one we enjoyed so much
as we ascended with other travelers way up
onto the loveliest of old-world islands.

II:
A Few Chickadees Alight in the Dying Light

How Chloé sees Atibi,
in a Dying Light

Anybody Home?

Opening the door, I wonder if you're still here,
then I wonder, just where is there, as I can't
find where you've just up and left, though
I wasn't invited, though you've asked me to go
along with your scheme years ago, and I didn't
as I didn't know what might be ahead, as in what
might happen if I stayed, but maybe someday,
not just what appears to be now, someday, sometime
I'll open our door, walk in and wonder what in
the world has changed, but then, it's such pain
that you've lived through, it seems to make sense
that you've gone, and I really don't mind that I've
not gone along for the lonely ride into a space
that no one, no one now knows where you are,
but you're someplace, right, someplace that I
have no possibility of ever visiting, as you just
have left what was here, though what was here
was such pain and misery, so it seems perfectly
clear why you're out there, even if I don't know
where your there is, but maybe that's not so
important now, even though, for all these years,
everything seemed so important, so I'll see what's
next, okay, and perhaps it's just taking a long walk,
but to where seems such a mystery, after all, we
took these walks ending up in Florence or Ixtapa,
and no one ever would think, that's not where we
are now, even though I sense you might still be here.

What Did You Just Say?

I'm not the disagreeable type, though lately, I seem to be most
disagreeable to what appears to be more and more for quite a
few out there, but in the end, and we know we'll all end, sooner
than some might expect, yet the next day, you know this, the next
day we can hardly remember what it was that got us into such a,
well, I was going to say what it was, but now I'm having so
much trouble remembering even that, and that seems to be
what we've been so worn out by, even though all of us are
harboring such seared nerve-ends that nobody knows quite
how to get us back to where we were when we started talking
back so quickly before the other, and now, we can't even
remember who the other was, though it was all so inconsequential,
but then, it was as if you, and I'm not saying you had anything
to do with this, but you started something awful bad way down
in a pretty frozen heart, and something lit that bloody organ so
that now, we've got not a spewing, not a barking, but one big
lava puke that just keeps pouring out, so much so, that we're
going to have to get out of the way, or we are just going to end
up like those nice Romans did way way back who are now just
a tourist stop for so many trying to find their way through ruins
of what was something not so bad, so long ago, but if we do
get out of the way, and not stuck into something terribly hot,
then one of us, and isn't that always the way it turns out, one
of us has got to start to clean up such a mess, even though
the mess is still steaming under our feet, pushing us further
and further away from what we're trying to keep from spreading
out any further into someone else's loving home, that if we
don't do something, well, and you know this, the whole town
where we are is going to just, how do you say it, go under,
and nobody really wants to go under over such a stupid thing
like, oh yeah, I did forget to bring home a gallon of milk,

or wine, or something harder that always goes down so easy.
And not to be so personal here, but I'd appreciate if you have
some time, to help me clean this up, for we have so little time
before someone else starts to have that volcanic eruptus, and
if we're not more careful, we'll all be memorialized in something
no one really knows what to call, but whatever it is, even if
somebody thinks it was just a simple what did you just say, well,
get over here, as we're going to need more brooms, more brooms.

So, We're All Going to Die, Right?

Every day I open the door, knowing how dangerous
a journey will be, but it is the world, even though
we have our own cosmos spinning right inside, here.
Once outside, however, I might last only fourteen more
days, as that's the timetable for asymptomatic commonly
called pre-death without having a clue when we'll just
fall down and convulse. But here's the thing, gas to go
anywhere is just around the corner offering cold beverages
to go, and who wants to turn down a cold beverage in these
times? Fruit and veggies and plant-based sausages are way
up the street, so I go out into this new world of microscopic
bugs sometimes just for the news not on-line, or coffee as
I'm no longer grinding beans on my own, or meds, and who,
who doesn't need tons of meds these days as new diagnoses
are developing so quickly, for all of us. Then there's the chance
of a walk or a walk and slow jog, but we're way past the day
when it was a pretty decent run, but that's long over, isn't it?
So sometimes, just to play it safe, I'll perch next to a double
window, scooting the chair as the Sun whirls across the skyline
which these days is very short as across the street we have
double deck houses, or two-story, for those not acquainted,
and then the houses on this side block out most of the afternoon
so I'm up early for any vitamin D rays on the short winter days.
Of course, we're not going to make it here for much longer,
and who would as brain, heart, lungs, and the terrible intestines
just can't keep up with all the pressure, the intensity of keeping
our various major and minor organs and connective tissues all
in sync, and who can do that forever even though some of us
never give this a very complete study, like now, when the sky
is so grey, all day, and sometimes the night seems *ad infinitum*
like we'll never ever see light again around here. But that's
a bit dramatic, isn't it? But think about it, how absolutely

beautiful it is to somehow wake from a dream, and there you
are, and everybody around the globe is wondering the very same
thing, here we go again, as weak and pitiful as I am, or you,
not that you're pitiful, but if you'd take a look, you'd know
what I'm looking at, but all that washes away if we splash
a little of that slightly cool water all over us, at least for some
who are keeping up with personal hygiene, and actually, some
are not, but I certainly didn't want to bring up anything that
might make matters worse, as they already are, aren't they?
So that's about it, and you were expecting some words of wisdom
to get you through the next day, but really, you'll be okay, but
then some of us won't, and that's sad, really, as who wants to
beam into one more Zoom funeral, or Shiva, or anything with
Zoom, but then, no worries, as we're assured someone else will
take care of all those details that we forgot to write out for our last
Zoom. Personally, and perhaps you might sense this, too, I'm quite
pleased to still be around, even though, and here it comes, we may
not all be here tomorrow, but enough of those gloomy the end is
near fears. You, how about you, what's going on with you? I was
afraid you might say that, but no worries, we'll come over with
something to nosh on, but on second thought, it's already dark,
and someone says it's quite late.

Now the Dying Who Are Almost Dead, Are Dead

The End? Well, we could hardly call it that, as if
whatever just happened, isn't found in an old
paper thin tome nobody's read for a zillion years.
Instead, the end, or The End, just keeps blistering
the heck out of nearly everyone, though some
are immune, and will never know when any End
is just around, looking for hopeless dopes like most
of us are now. Prayers done with, floors mopped
with Clorox, as if that would scare anyone away,
but the Bugs like that deep inhalation we take when
we walk into any room, like sniffing lighter fluid
right into the lungs where it plans to stay and stay
until all of us are turned over onto our stomachs
by the kindest of medical staff, hoping the deep
breaths will pull us out, but most of us have already
died, and had no clue anything was like The End as
so many are whispering about now, as if Breaking
News isn't about a new political cataclysm, but rather
breaking the hearts of so many in so many hugely
different parts of our world, everywhere even in
Antarctica, and who brought the Bugs in to such a
pristine, icy world anyway? ICUs are now in gift
shops, chapels, parking lots with unique tenting
materials and refrigerator trucks behind and out
of sight, keeping all the dead quite cool until we
find a place that will prepare the dead without
ending up as the prepared dead. That's our new
world with the best hopes of looking ahead nearly

two or three years out, and even then, new varieties
will awaken all of us again, those who aren't quite
living any more, but just waiting, you know for what
don't you, call it what you want, but here, it's The End.

A Few Chickadees Alight in the Dying Lilacs

Who really knows about these things as so many
are so deeply absorbed by what they are calling
some bad bugaboo, but it's probably more the
sense of just being discombobulated, out of whack,
adrift, a pensive look into space that never changes,
and then, along come a few chickadees, flitting
branch to branch, and then like we knew, landing
so far away we'll never see the miracle of wing,
color, the tiny tweeting of such a delicate sight,
but then, that's what we're trying to get through,
right, the constant grey storm clouds bringing
more, and everyone in the neighborhood is so
positive about this, saying such niceties as we
really needed that, or it's good for the ground
water, or next year the cherries will blossom
like nothing ever, but if it rains too hard and too
fast, most of us without those new fangled
roof gutters will be down in the basement
brooming all those streams of water toward
the sewer drain, though more streams start
anew right where the chimney starts next
to the heater, but then, the rain or whatever
it is that may come down upon us let's up
a bit, and then we'll go upstairs for something
that might refresh and take the weight off
of all that we are wondering about here,
though just down the road, nothing is going
on like it's going on here, nope, nothing and
that's just about what it's like whether it's

bad bugs killing millions of us off like a plague,
or too much snow or too much rain, or a
dizzying hail storm that we'll save for our
grandkids, unless, of course, they've up and left.

When & If

After *Shiva,* after *Shloshim,* perhaps I'll start wandering again,
or, I may go down into the basement and wonder what
to do with so many dresses, blouses, coats, shoes, but
in time, they may all soon disappear just as you have, though
we all knew the day that we couldn't remember would ever
be like she's just up and left us kind of day, but then, just
like that, you up and took off, to wherever off is, if it is any-
where nearby, but all of us don't know about that too much.
With luck, I might sail away somewhere on an old steamer,
looking for Orson, or Sydney, or Rita from so many old classic
movies that helped us through long nights, and lovely afternoons.
I'll need to pack a tuxedo, for every now and then, we're asked
to dress up, though I don't have much interest in what you loved
so much, but I'm not even sure I'd still fit in what I once fitted
into very nicely, but now, nothing feels worth all those buttons
and shiny shoes. We'll see, and perhaps that's all we'll be ever
able to see, just a vague grey day ahead of one after another.
Perhaps walking through all the floors of the British Museum
might help, or not, as not everything appeals as it once did
back then, when we discovered Lao Tzu with his ox behind a
slightly smudged glass home and hut, where he still gazes into
the future, for all of us. What does the old sage wonder about
now, but then, it might not matter as we have another museum
scheduled for tomorrow, as well as trips on the water boats
taking us to more and more places to walk around just to gaze.
The Colosseum and the Forum might not seem so oh look at that,
now that there's no one to look with at what once was Rome ages
ago, but then we're all older, aren't we, and wondering into
an age we'll probably regret, but not before standing somewhere
in Florence, wondering which floor of the Uffizi to start with first,
but that may not be such a problem, as by now, I'm starting to

even wonder where I might be if I'm here or over there, as even
my old brain, once a font of wisdom and delight, now has turned
into a bit of a muddle, though the old corpse could be worse off,
but not today, not just yet, something more to see we once saw
sometimes in shorts and sundresses, sometimes in something
else, sometimes with nothing else, but then, we'll sail out into
the Mediterranean, and climb one of the picturesque islands
and for the afternoon, all we'll do is enjoy the salad and wine,
even if no one thinks of ever saying, may we join you, and of
course, I say certainly, and then, just like that, the sky is sunnier.

> O soothest Sleep! if so it please thee, close
>   in midst of this thine hymn my willing eyes
>
> —John Keats

It's late in the afternoon, but then, about this time,
it's always late in the afternoon, and though I'm about
to fall out of this old chair, propping me up high enough
to see what is going on outside, that is if I open the blinds
just enough to let the dying light in to light up whatever
is inside here, though lately, I'm not so certain there's
that much to light up, as the dim light is so much preferred,
don't you think? But then you're not here, right, and you'll
probably never come by as you're busy over there probably
doing nothing, as I'm doing nothing here, but isn't that the
way it goes, we're both doing nothing, including anyone
who's just popped into the scene to see if anything we aren't
doing would be more interesting than what anyone else is
doing that's interesting, but that's our conundrum, isn't it,
and to tell you the truth, all of us are probably just doing
nothing right now, and if anybody calls up, or texts us, we'd
say we're plenty busy, but why is it that we need to tell so
many that we're on to something big, or even bigger, when
we don't really have anything interesting going on, except
watching the dying light get just a bit dimmer where we are,
but perhaps that's all we can expect, that we're not freezing,
we're not all banged up after an armed robbery, we're still
able to put together syllables and phonemes, we can swallow,
thank heavens, but lately, we've been swallowing a lot more
of that white/red bottled water as the evening slowly descends
into dusk, and then, that's about it, isn't it, and we've had such

a terrific day by not succumbing to whatever is so easy to just
let the old scythe right in, as there's really not that much more
to do, but the covers seem inviting, and perhaps we'll know
what we can do if we can only make it through O soothest Sleep!

Not Generalizable, But That Doesn't Matter, Does It?

Today we've learned we have all gained half a pound in every ten days,* but it's a limited study, and we're still about the same, but the good news is that all those pounds are not generalizable, and that's what's so fascinating, not the pounds, not the carry-outs, not the countless wine bottles, not the endless pizza boxes but notably, none of this is generalizable, and sure, some of you out there are more familiar with what can and cannot be generalized, but generalizable, really, has it really come down to this, and perhaps that's not so bad, but let's hope everything else in the world is not generalizable either, for who could handle that kind of world data information where even though the study is limited, but still quite valuable, it's not, that's right, generalizable, so our neighbors, of course, may have actually gained more than .6 of a pound every 10 days, but we're relieved we certainly did not, even though we're still in hibernation, still not fully immune, still confined to a few rooms which continually become smaller and smaller, but thankfully some dear friends reminded us we're going to make it, and that more than anything is probably the best generalizable factor, but of course, we know that's not true, not at all, as so many social diseases afflicted by half the population may never make it unless someone starts unloading quarrelsome behaviors that in the end make just staying alive a few more days something of a miracle,
yes?

*The New York Times 3/23/2021 A8 "How Much Did We Gain," Para. 11/line 3

Just Not Yet

Tonight, like so many nights, we spoke again about
possibly letting go, and moving on through the universe,
but we both know we don't know anything about
these plans, which are really not plans, as everyone
might already know, but the only thing we may know
is that someday, something like this will happen, of
course, but not soon, as that would surprise both of
us, but sometime soon, though now we're just trying
to make it back and forth to little rooms without further
slipping up, but little by little, we can both tell something
is changing, and that something is something we want
to pay attention to, but we don't want to pay attention
to it, as we're more interested in lunch plans and an
afternoon of old movies which we never would have
imagined long ago, but now they provide some kind of
delight, though delight is not something what the other
might express when and if something happens, but not
yet, of course, we know that, but still, it's something
that starts to linger with both of us, but for now, nothing
is happening that we want to be alarmed about, just not
yet.

Then, There's That

Of course, no one expected what would happen happen just
like that, but isn't that the way most of our well-laid plans
end up, so surprisingly different than what anyone would
have ever imagined, but why, for heaven's sake, did anyone
think things would go just as we planned back then, even if
back then was so long ago, though no one even has any notes
to see exactly what everyone got so horribly wrong, but then,
almost everyone, not everyone, goes into shaking-head
syndrome, and a kind of pitiful laugh saying, well it really
wasn't as bad as we thought it was going to be, in fact,
it could have been so much worse, but now, no one wants
to even commiserate on how awful awful that could have
been, how could they, for don't they know that no one,
no one really has any idea how any of this will end up.

Deep Deep Space

So then, one evening, or was it yesterday, she left
on her way through the darkest of space, but not
at all caring a bit, and though she did say something
about the cold, and might need a ton of blankets,
well, who knows how everyone is covered up these
days as the place out there really isn't out there, is
it? Of course not, but it's nice to think so, especially
if you think that's what's out there, but I doubt if
anything is out there, don't you, but don't take it
personally, for these kinds of remarks bring out the
worst for some who know exactly what's out there.
But now it's just one of us, and of course we're talking
to ourselves so that makes two of us inside the one
of us, but we're having all kinds of roller-coaster ups
and downs and tilt-a-whirls, if that makes sense, and as
well, I wonder why so many rattlesnakes are shaking
their tails, so I'm facing extreme danger, but then, of
course, they're all in my head, and really not there,
just like they were really not there when Harrison
Ford said I really don't like snakes, and to be honest,
I really don't like snakes either, as there were a bunch
of bad copperheads at one of our Boy Scout overnights
and that was something I'm still talking to therapists
about, but they're slowly slipping out of my brain,
and right now, I'm looking at all these clothes closets
and they seem to be pretty horrifying as well as nobody
can even step into the dark closest and remove anything
as everything is squeezed so tightly together that there's
no way we're going to remove even that beautiful blue
one you loved so much, and nearly always wore to our
trips to the ballet on Sundays. But now there are no more
trips, no more Londons or Florences, or Cozumel beaches.

I can't think of anywhere I could go without thinking
who's not here, oh, of course, it's you in your own space
suit way out there, and heck, not even caring a hoot or
two about who needs to breathe out there, anyway, so
I guess that's about it, and don't worry, this will happen
to you, too, just wait, don't worry, perhaps it will never
ever happen, but according to the obits in the local paper,
well, you'll figure it out, unless you hold your breath
and pretend all of this is balderdash but you'll know,
how soon, well soon enough as they say, soon enough.

As Time Goes By

A sigh is just a sigh.
—Herman Hupfeld

Some of us may have made it, or we at least pretend
we have made it, though all of us know we're just
kidding ourselves, but what else is there now that
a few of us can fill our lungs without stinging bats
that somehow did not find their way down into us.
We could also take the next hour (day) (week) (year)
to remember all those who have fallen, who did not
know what in the world was inside of them, but it
was inside them, and many who were nearby have
also fallen down, some in the most hopeless places
of the world, and as well, some in the most luxurious
rooms not everyone could dream about, but still,
it might do us all some good to just remember what
none of us could ever imagine happening, just like
that.

"... if not now, when?"

—Hillel the Elder in *Pirkei Avot*

For Dearest Jacqueline
(March 11, 1944–July 3, 2021)

The night is close by, slowly climbing up our insides
and nobody no one wants to do anything but let
the storm storm into our bodies, for isn't that what
we all want, something foreign to take us away
from all our troubles, but most of us are not miserable,
as we just think we are, waiting it out for the event
which we so wanted to attend, but we're not attending,
are we, as now we're lying down, quite supine, but
not in an ethereal sense, more in a transitioning from
one to another, from active hoorahs to active dying, so
we're just going to keep breathing, however shallow
that may seem, for after breathing, there's only ash
and that ash, if we can call what we once were, is now
what's left of what we all were so keen on, on loving.

O Beatrice

The image of her when she starts to smile
breaks out of words, the mind cannot contain it,
a miracle too rich and strange to hold.
                              —Vita Nuova XXI

A long time ago, in Florence, away from the Masters,
I wandered into a tiny room, a chapel, once reserved
for Beatrice, but she's long gone, isn't she, and no one
sits with me, and no one came in behind me, and for
a moment, I did not ever want to move away from
this dark place for I've never been so close, even
reading something so divine, than here with Dante,
but sensing my wife might be waking in the late
morning light, I started to wander back to our tiny
room, but not before stopping for a cappuccino.
So some of the days, like now, when I'm sitting
next to her deathbed, I'm wondering just where
can I go in this world, knowing no one is where
someone might be, eyes opening in the morning
light, perhaps like Beatrice might have, right before
she told her Dante not to be afraid, to step into the light.

Right as Rain

Today, the longest day by the way, and thinking about all
the days going way back, but I'm not lonely, which of course
could be total denial, but all who do know me think that
too, but I'd like to believe I'm just alone, and I'm okay
with that. Alone a lot. Sort of like an old tree, oak maybe,
though I'm not scheduled yet for death and destruction,
but everyone else is talking about a possible trim at the
top, as a few dead branches have started to appear.
But still, I'm standing, somewhat tall, taller really than
all the others on the block, though we all know not
for long. I'm also pretty much alone in the pool even if
there's two of us lapping back and forth, or worse,
a third, and I'm standing or lying over in the corner
in the yoga studio, and no one ever thinks of coming
over and getting into one's space, unless something
needs correcting, and I'm corrected often, so someone
does come over and moves a foot just slightly, or an
arm or a hip, depending, of course. I'm eating alone
now, and dining still like the gentleman I hope I've been,
not gulping, like my cat always does, down in a flash.
Movies now are mostly in the dark. Dreams are still
in the dark, reclined and probably snoring loudly,
and there's no one to recognize, but sometimes there's
you, who wants to drop in every now and then.
No one reads over my shoulder the news, or reads
aloud a headline I'm not reading. No one answers
the phone anymore, not even me, as I've given up

on all the unidentified spams. You're picking up
a theme, right, and you're worried I'm too alone,
even if that's a preference, like Bartleby, but I see
you all out there, but I'm just not going to come over
and blab on for who knows how long with you, as
I just couldn't. But if I saw a hint of a smile, or a
totally unexpected hello there, okay, I'm right here,
I'll be right over. I'm okay, really, right as rain.

III:
Sitting Shiva

Hang in There

Just where, as I'd really prefer not to hang anywhere,
either by my fingernails on a window ceiling where
I'm slowly slipping off the fine window frame that
others probably put their elbows on over the years
just to gaze out at whatever scene or season it might
be, but I'm not exactly looking out I'm looking back
in to see if anybody might drop by after hearing my
constant yelling for help, but who wants to break
into a private residence on the hunch that somebody
might need a hand, as I am about to fly away from
here, and though aerial flight is something I've always
wondered about, going that way without propellers,
or engine thrusters, or heck, even a parachute or
a bungee rope but no, I've got nothing above, on, or
nearby that might help in the extremely swift descent
onto a hard landing, but that's not what you meant,
right, you only were wishing that despite some tragedy
in someone else's life, you shouldn't have to go that
route as well, so yes, it's something that means well,
but all I can still think about is just where do you propose
I throw the rope as we have no banisters on the second
floor that might do well for a single-story descent with
a quick snap and bounce that might take away all the
woes we have, but heck, I've still got stuff to do, really,
and most of it is something I'd better get done as no
one really wants to look at a busy, stuffed to the gills
house with way too much to get rid of, so no, I'd rather
not even think about option B, and since all our windows
are really only a few feet from the ground up, well,
there would be no time to really get the bungee bounce,
or the parachute to even open, or enough time to descend
before the slight noose tightens around the old throat,

so no thanks, I'm good, I was up in an upside-down hand
stand this morning, like many mornings, but that's a lot
more interesting than just stepping off into the wild
blue yonder, so, much appreciated as some might say,
but hold off please with all the hang-in-there please, please.

Sitting Shiva

For Jacqueline Clinton
(March 11, 1944–July 3, 2021)

We're back from the ash factory, though we're not
exactly a we anymore, are we, and we'll somehow
figure out where who is where, but for now, there's
just the other, or as some would say, the widower,
which sounds something like gazing out a window,
and, of course, that's right, but looking won't help
too much in this case, so we'll light a glassy candle,
and find a stool or two, but then, the other isn't
sitting, right, just the one. By early evening then,
mourners will drop in or by, and most don't want
to hear about poor Job's *tsuris,* as everybody reads
something from it sometime in a lifetime, and then,
others will read *Job* later, for the other. Long prayers,
sad faces, and then somebody pours something
no one has seen in ages, and all cry out *l'chaim.*
We'll repeat six more evenings if we can last that
long, or for the more reformed, three might do
and by then, we'll need to find where all the
plastic boxes are for all the kugels and knishes,
and even a few dishes in Pyrex we can't even
identify. Soon we'll be walking around the block,
a sign of returning to some semblance of life,
though we'll be pondering just how we can carry
on knowing how we're missing what once was you.

Then, Nothing

Certainly not a black hole, that would be way too too
even though that's what it is, despite that it couldn't
be just that, but obviously something terribly not
that can no longer heal or renew what's left of herself,
if you know what I mean, and of course you don't,
for no one answered all those Can You Help Me
Please appeals, not just occasionally, but every
day, all the time, so often, even I was losing whatever
it was that I once had, and now I don't have and
wouldn't mind at all answering a few of those
troubles, but they've all blown out the window
so to speak, paper requests floating in the gusts
across such a vast space and the fact that it's
pitch black doesn't help at all in retrieving even
one of the slips, demands, or hollering screams
as now all that there is, from what I can tell, is then,
nothing.

The Plan

It's the where and how I wonder about, don't you,
but then, who's worrying about stuff like that far
out, or away, as we all hope that's too far away
to even think about something like that, but we
do, don't we, and we pretend whatever the situation,
we'll be on some white sand beach, or viewing all
of Paris from way above, with no worries, none
at all, but then, when and if that time does come
I doubt any of us will be able to even board a flight
for anywhere, though that's always the plan, isn't
it, and of course it's nice to think that way as it
gives us such great big sighs knowing we're never
going to be that bad off, but from what I've seen
out there, it is going to not only be bad but very
Bad as in Bad Bad much much worse than slipping
out into the universe, all so tiny, wailing for air
and of course, food, and then a whole lifetime
we hope of fine friendships, fine wine, fine every-
thing, and who wouldn't want that even now, right?

Yes, Dear, Only I Didn't Say Yes, Dear

Someone whispers tenderness so softly, I can barely
hear, then I realize it's just me, talking to the actors
on the screen where a father says goodbye to a son,
and that young son reaches up to embrace who he
knows will never come back, ever, for now he's certain
papa is another of those who are so crazily brave,
setting their lives on fire just to be able to resist,
and of course, that's what the movie is about, but
here I am wondering where was any tenderness
when all I was doing was providing solace, comfort,
knowing but not knowing someone who I probably
did not offer enough kindness to, as the request was
simply to open the blinds, I'd like some water, why
were you gone so long it seemed so long you were
gone, but really, I wasn't gone long, only a few minutes.
Now there's no you, just you whispering turning
me into someone who is just there to take requests,
and then, of course, now there's no one making
such requests, so in a moment or two, I'll probably
leave you with what you have left to offer everyone
out there, but perhaps we will meet, toast not only
to who we are now, but to all those we've almost
left behind, and now we know we don't know
who that could possibly be, but perhaps we can
help each other remember, briefly, their kindness.

It's Time, My Dear

For Bonnie Lewis, music therapist

Some say, especially those who drop in to play pleasant songs,
say musical chords can actually cross the corpus collosum,
that wonderful band of neurons that help those who are not here
for long to enjoy what's left of what's not going to be here,
for long, the one in the bed, not the one who is strumming
a guitar in hopes of lifting someone's heart just slightly so that
whatever is left, both the right and the left can enjoy some
kind of wonderful synapse that helps the one in bed to say
all is okay, I'm almost dead, but whatever you strum on the
strings, I'm with you, leaving earth anytime soon, but so glad
you stopped by to provide solace and comfort and perhaps
that's all we can do, as we help our elders to prepare for the
long journey into elsewhere, wherever elsewhere is, as if
anyone really knows, but that depends, of course, what
the preacher said on Sunday, or the rabbi on Saturday,
and whether anybody ever believes we're travelling
to a special place, and of course we are, for who wouldn't
want to be expected in some special space that no one knows
about, but everyone, not exactly everyone, but those who believe,
it's just the beyond the beyond, wherever that might ever
be, but we'll hum along, maybe even join in to the old
music that makes us feel as though we're not really dying
here, in this bed all the insurance is paying for, but perhaps
it's just as good as any place any of us might want to be
when someone whispers, it's time, my dear, it's time.

Knock Knock, Who's There?

Minding my own business, trying to stay asleep though
up much earlier, but now safe under a pile of covers,
then, out of nowhere, "Are you out there somewhere?"
in her voice, which is what some call voice recognition,
or at least we call it that when we think we know just
who is making this dream call in morning before morning
if we really want to call 3:15 an early morning wake-up
and yes, I'm awake all right, wouldn't you if you knew
nobody can say anything like that if somebody is officially
boxed away as cremains, awaiting a scattering, as some
might say, on a yahrzeit that is still so far away that no
one yet, to my knowledge, has even thought about flight
tickets so we can all gather by the harbor where you've
requested a final scattering, not the traditional unveiling
as there's certainly no stone, and nothing under the stone
but that's really not important now, is it, but can you just
explain, neatly, without starting into something longwinded
about what dreams are really about, could you just say
no worries, bro, that stuff is out there, and might even
return, not to scare you at all, really, but just to leave you
completely, totally, like never ever before, totally gaga.

Who Isn't Thinking Like That, Like You?

After Gerald Stern, "Behaving Like a Jew"

Someone said a day ago or was it a century
ago somewhere in Vilnius, start behaving
like a Jew who you are, and then I remembered
O yes, I'm already wearing black most every
day, and I have a black hat I love, but don't
wear except for funerals, and black shoes
I only wear to concerts and even black
socks, and I'm not eating anything with scales,
and stopped with those pork chops so very
long ago, and was trying to recall even Esther's
story in The Book of Esther how almost all
of the Jews in old old Persia were going up
in smoke, but thank G-d for the Queen, and it
goes on and on like these little memories
that flash in and out on occasion, of course,
not when I'm doing something like trying
to remember the Eight-fold Path, or old
Epictetus trying to save the poor and weary
from all the hordes and all the famines that
tend to make any Roman anxious, and who,
pray tell, who is not anxious in times like
these, and what other times are there
other than now, that is if we only live
here and now, not then and over there,
just like an old brother now with plaque
attaching itself to more and more of
his old dendrites, who said just the other day,
or was it half a century ago, What To Do?
only he hadn't invented that, no,
just saying what he learned to say
in New Delhi when a consternation all
of a sudden just grips someone like
that, grips, as in *Oy Vey,* Heavens to

Betsy, and yes you have had those
days, don't kid me, and if you haven't
what's wrong with you, most of us
are down here in the basement
sorting through decades of boxes
set aside for someone else to
downgrade, or was it downsize,
I, for one, keep getting those two
mixed up, like most everything
I know keeps getting mixed up until
all I can do is ascend the stairs
and bring out a pot and boil more
of those green little marbles the
kind most say they hate, but
really, roasted, broiled, boiled,
baked, who, who wouldn't
want to eat something from all
places like Brussels, wherever
Brussels is where so many make
so many sprouts so green, so lovely
green, but for you know whose sake,
please don't overcook them as
no one really wants soft food
like that, unless of course we're
already eating soft food and
occasionally it's acceptable,
but we don't want to start
habits like that that we can
never dissuade ourselves of,
and who doesn't want to dis-
suade one's aging self from
one's aging self, unless, of
course, you don't even know
that's already been happening

for ages now, or perhaps just
a few months, but everybody
I know, and you, too, admit it,
everybody around here is a
little more aged than they were
even just a few years ago,
and that's where we are all
headed, but no one, no one
you know or knows briefly, really
wants to be persuaded, as in now
Dear One, we think this would
be such a good place for you
as they play checkers every night
and on Wednesdays everybody
sings old songs nobody ever
sings again for who in whose
mind would ever want to
do that, yes, that, as if you should
pay more attention and stop
behaving like you have been
even if, even if you are a Jew
and who, who isn't acting like
that already and if not, just wait,
you'll see soon enough and then
before you know it, and yes that's
going to be a big disappointment,
well, how do we say this so you
won't take it badly, but you will
of course, like you always do,
but here's the thing, you're just
too late, and that's a good thing,
right, but then we'll all sing together,
Roy and Dale's happy, "Happy Trails,"
but then you'll be gone, like, forever

and who, who wants to lead a Shiva
like that when we were just beginning
to like what was part of our world, now
gone, forever and forever, really,
forever.

So

My dear, where exactly are you, as someone suggested
Venus, but please know it's much colder there even
if we turn our thermostats up a bit for now it's much
colder than when you left us, and even then, we weren't
that sure you knew you were leaving for planets far
beyond our reach, and it's not that we wanted to go
where you were going, but even though Venus is
so much out there, and even though we know how
cold it is out there none of us truly wanted to go
where we think you are, but we have no real
wondering at all as to where you really are as you
might not be who we so lovingly remembered who
you were, or who we hoped you might be in all your
wardrobes that simply astounded us, but then, now,
all we have is what you were and wondering where
in the universe have you found a peaceful home even
though we know that's way too much for us to imagine
even ever briefly, as we know you've taken flight but
all of us here are gazing far into the night sky wondering
if that star, or perhaps one of those bright planets
which we see brightening the night sky is where you
now call home, even if we are here at home, missing you
so.

On Fire

Right there, right there in the middle of such a long blathering
that no one imagined could go on longer and longer, but of course,
the words just spilled out, over and over, more and more, and then,
out of nowhere, the beautiful, the one phrase I've been waiting
for forever, as it so perfectly described those wonderful New York
characters who never, ever, learned how to stop blathering so,
the lovely, "yada, yada, yada," and right then, I wanted to stop
the person suffering, going over and over such painful memories
as we were all in such an *angst* group, going around and around
with such *tsuris* inside of us, waiting our turn like children hoping
we might be able to get just a word in to say something that will
help us to even be able to stand and move away from this dark
circle, head home, saying I'm home, anyone home, and of course,
no one is home, as the loved one has gone, not down the street
for an errand, or to sip coffee with a dear friend and catch-up,
no gone, as in gone for good, as in not here, as in never again, so
why then, why does it do anyone anywhere anytime to say those
lovely coming home words, hoping for a reply, even a quiet one,
and then, how perfect, the lonely Siamese lifts his head off of a
perch we set in the window for him to whine so pitifully when
birds fly by but, where was I, do you remember, isn't that telling
us something about how we're all down in a sinkhole, no ropes,
no ladders, no E.M.T. guys dressed as if we're all on fire, but
of course, we are, but not the good kind of fire, just the kind
that keeps blowing ash all over our faces and fingers for so long
now, how can we stand it, and then, O G-d, we're standing,
and saying goodbye, see you next week, I can't wait to tell you
how I must have been a bad mother, I'm so lonely, and me, heck,
I don't think I even had a sentence out before someone jumped
in and said what has been aching in her heart for so long, but
it's like this, over and over, blathering on, yada, yada, yada.

After "Insomnia"

after Elizabeth Bishop

And it ends so sweetly, especially
since we've never ever been
properly introduced or for that
matter, introduced at all, but then,
who of us have those rare moments
that begin, in innocence with, I'd like
to, but then, the moment fades
like Elizabeth fades as well when
she writes "and you love me,"
and after that I'm so in love,
wondering how she knows how
I've waited forever, even if it's only
a bird whispering, but then, the one
I lost, she'd say that every day, but
not "you love me," but I love you,
and now there's no moment left
to echo, yes dear, I love you, too,
even after you just up and left
for places so far away in dark space,
a place none of us ever want
to travel to, though there you are,
out there, floating so peacefully
in that icy cold space some of us
are so afraid to visit, the space
where you are, even though we
knew what love was, yes, you'd
say I love you over and over in your
last days though I never wanted
to say it right after you, and now
in your "far and way beyond sleep,"

well, please know I'm losing more
and more of these precious dreams
some say all of us might want more
of in this all-new inverted world.

Troubled

Knowing you, you'll probably ask where the heck am I now
though I'm even wondering about where that might be,
but somebody out of the blue just asked where are you,
and of course, that's probably me, wondering how you're
doing out there, cold as hell, as some might say, but of
course, that's ridiculous as we both agreed that was some
fabrication of the Ancient Ones who wanted a place to go
to when and if they succumbed to living far too long, but
I'm just wondering how you are doing, especially as I heard
you wondering about in my lonely old brain, but just so you
know, I'm pulling through, with the help of loving friends
who say nothing about why or how you died, and that's
quite good, in fact, for I have no idea how that happened
myself, so I appreciate the vague innuendoes, if that is
acceptable to all out there, and just exactly who is all out
there, for sometimes I'm just sitting where I'm sitting,
and of course I know I should be out and about making
a way toward our lovely Lake Park, but even if I did that,
I'm quite certain you're not coming back, even though
you seem to visit occasionally when I'm least expecting
visitors, and I'm surprised that you're even calling so late
though it's quite understandable, but just exactly how are
you making these calls, as I'll admit they're quite disturbing
as someone has reminded me you're long gone, way out
in the universe, wherever that might be, and who of course
knows anything about where anybody goes when they leave
as you left, but now it's so hard to try to visit how you left
that afternoon, not talking a bit, not breathing a bit, not
moving at all, heck it was almost as if this was your last day
on earth, and I just walked into your room, not our room,
just your room, and there you were, reclining, mouth open
for just a bit of air, but no air coming in to you, dear, as we

discovered you're gone, as in out of here, as in gone, gone,
which none of us knew what that meant, and a gentle figure
arrived with a stethoscope though now I'm certain everyone
knew you'd left for good, but now we're going to try to prepare
you for the event you never thought might occur that you're
already gone, out in space, as some say, though heaven is
such a speculative wonder as we talked about it quite often
long before you left us all, and then, well, we waited and
waited and waited as it was dark into Shabbat and no one
was able to come and take you away for a long restful night
in a place I'd rather not even think as a final B&B final home,
but there you were, out of sight, perhaps in the basement,
alone, as you often were, left alone on the gurney, waiting
for a final burning just as you requested, and now, months
later, I'm still wondering where in the universe are you so
please let me know as you can tell can't you, I'm so very
troubled.

So So, So Let's Order Carry-Out

But not terribly not so so, or hugely so so, just sort of so so
though few will know what in the world is that, but then
not everyone has such a clown smile on for special effects,
and perhaps when the door is closed, and no one is watching,
perhaps the lips tighten slightly, just daring that somebody
somewhere, somehow, some way might start shouting to
the rooftops just like when "Beale" shouts in "Network," and
you know the lines don't you, it's pretty much how all of us
feel about now, fed up with just about everything that's
going on, and not going on, so go ahead, say it in your head,
"I'm as mad as hell, and I'm not going to take this anymore!"
except we're probably going to take it just like we've been
taking it, and probably will for a very long time way into
the future, but that sounds a bit lame, doesn't it, as if
we have no real future, even if as the ancient priests
wondered whether the Sun would return after seeing it
disappear, so let's get up early and pray a lot hoping the
best for light, and if the light doesn't return, let's just
go back to bed, as the lights are still out, not only outside,
but inside, as the stars aren't even blinking every now
and then, though we're hopeful, of course, but for what
none of us are quite sure of as so much has been such a
huge disappointment, but hey, did you say it was time
for adult refreshments, indeed, so let's order carry-out.

A Simple Zero-Sum Conundrum

Two (or 2 if you like) take away One, (okay 1 it is)
usually results in the happy arithmetic of 1 (or One)
and no one really has any business, mathematically,
to say otherwise, but in other universes, such as ours,
where two live as one, (1), the absence of the other
(other 1), either suddenly or prolonged, results in an
altogether calculation of not ever understanding that
which has been in place for so long, so anyone knows
if one takes away half of what was whole, the whole is
now not a whole of two, but a questionable whole of
one, and yes, you saw this coming, right, how can the
one be whole when the new one whole used to be, or
shortly ago, a twosome, not a onesome, as who in their
right minds would look at two and think one, but to
continue, can't we have the lovely comment that so
many make even if it's uncalled for, for what do
onlookers really know, but as you might expect, even
though appearances are not what they are, even despite
that, someone looking from afar will say, smiling, aren't
they a lovely couple, holding hands like that, arm in arm
like that, smooching in places we usually do in private,
but of course, that's a whole different conundrum of what
the onesome is doing not as a twosome, but as something
someone might say, they're whole, not apart, at least not
in public, but now, after staring into the grave for who
knows how long, there's only one going home, and the
comfy greeting of Honey, I'm home, doesn't seem to
appeal as it once did, though there is comfort when a pet
awakens or stretches or shakes in such a way that they
may think you are planning a walk, or a feeding, but
really, you're not, and now, even though you're a one,
there's so much in the house, in drawers, in closets, in

the basement, on hangers, in extra clothes closets, on
chairs, well, someone else is living here, of course, but
of course, someone is also not living here, so let's see
where we are so far, as this will continue until the one
one day just isn't going to know today is another math
problem that no one will solve except all those who
once knew the two, then the one, and then, oh please,
you did take arithmetic, yes, so two (2), minus 1 (one)
equals one until the one subtracts into not another, but
yes, that's right, and it's not even zero, just an anti-zero,
so that's where we're going, even though none here like
the numbers, even though the numbers, always, and again,
always are always right, right?

Reading "Joy of Wine," With Li Ch'ing-Chao to the Tune of "A Dream Song," Many Centuries Later, Near a Great Lake

Ages ago, so long ago, we travelled north
to see migrating birds, and the colors so
brilliant even as they floated to the ground,
but we found a table at the Fox & Hounds,
and after, of course I made a wrong turn,
and then, completely lost in the dark dark
woods, but even without a GPS to guide
us out and home, somehow we found a way
south still a bit tipsy, not far from the Lake
with so many Canadians settling into the late
night, and the waves were crashing onto
the beach near our small home, and pulling
onto the street where only one of us lives
now, we startled grazing deer on our lawn,
and then, quite late, we found a lonely bed.

Goodnight All, Sweet Dreamy Dreams

For Linda Murphy, sage burner

Sage is burning in the house now, waving
and blowing softly to keep a small wisp
of smoke rising into the corners, just like
when we lifted the lulav and etrog
to welcome Sukkot, though now we are
cleansing the rooms, even the basement,
from whatever is making such terrifying
nightmares, pokes in the night, loud
accusations of Where did you go,
When will you be back, Why are you
not speaking to me, and at first I was
certain you were yelling those impossible
to answer puzzles, but perhaps it was me,
perhaps I was poking me in the back,
fast asleep, then you, then me waking
way too early to be waking at all, so
terrified someone was here with me,
who couldn't be with me, here, now.
The two of us now waving sage, burning
smoke, reading Sanskrit, turning the
wood inside the yoga singing bowl,
removing from this house all that
is broken, chipped, scratched, warped,
so we wave, relight, wave, relight, as
we are here to wave what's now left
until it stops glowing in the early
evening light in this house. Goodnight
all, sweet dreamy dreamy dreams.

An Elucidation on Death and Dying

Not dead yet, as the happy phrase goes,
though we are wondering about this, yes,
as who hasn't been wondering about this,
yes, so really, perhaps we shouldn't be
so worked up, stressed out about this
as sooner or later, and let's hope it is,
as sooner or later, conscious with a big
scream or just fading away as so many
do these days either in hospice or the
other option is that everyone stopped
coming around to check up on you-know-
who, so then it's possible, isn't it, that
we will request another year as there's
so much to still get done, right, as there's
always so much to get done, and who
would take care of this, the basement,
the attic, and before you know it, a
highly paid team will be carrying just
about everything out to the curb with
or without our permission, and it's
really okay, isn't it, as now we can't
use all the still unused appliances,
dishes, blankets, forgotten letters
which needed replies, and all those
photographs perhaps someone
might send them all to the local
library, or on a terribly misguided
hunch, the local historical society,
but no, let's get something straightened
out, shall we, it's just not going
to matter anymore, is it, so can
you all say this with me in unison,

it's just not going to matter anymore
is it, but of course, there are a few
who will whimper or worse, sob
their way out of this, but really,
soon we'll be gone, and then
that's just it, we won't have to
worry about getting more time
to finish up everything that needs
to be finished up, and that's
all right, isn't it, isn't it, at
least for now if any one of us
really knows what now is when
soon now will not be now, ever.

Burial at Sea

We're sailing now, a sunset sail, friends
who knew all three, as we've brought
what's left of our very dear ones, one
a husband, another a mother with a
daughter aboard, and a wife, with a
husband aboard, and as soon as the
sun is about to set, we will start opening
bags of bone and ash, and begin to say
prayers, perhaps an Our Father, perhaps
a solo, and a Kaddish for the wife, so all
can finally come to rest not in old graveyards,
but somewhere in the deep cold waters,
somewhere where we'll probably never
be able to sail ourselves back for others,
careful to note the direction of the evening
wind, who's already lifting shot glasses, all
a bit tipsy, careful not to join our departed,
then a repast for all, and by nightfall, we'll
scatter back to our lonely homes, remembering
this beautiful summer night where we all cried
goodbyes, remembering where we were that
lovely summer evening sailing out into the bay.

Wouldn't That Be Something?

Then, dear ones, we have moments we just
have no explanation for, no reasoned moments
that might pull us all out of this brink we've
fallen into so absentmindedly, but perhaps
this is all we can expect, a moment with you,
well, it was more than a moment, wasn't it,
and now we're wondering about new fields
of French lavender, and yes, we've never quite
imagined ourselves here, but just so you know,
it's quite enjoyable, perhaps so much more
than anyone ever expected, and we're both
good with that, yes, so perhaps we do want
what each of us has, a longing, even though
we've longed for so many in our lovely past,
but seeing you just then, so unexpectedly like
that, and by the end of the evening, there we
were, holding hands for the first time, as if
we've known each other all this time, so yes,
let's go to Paris soon and drink some of that
dark green absinthe the two of us have heard
so much about, but not so much as we'll never
be able to lift ourselves up to each other and ask,
let's go way up there so we can see all that's
below as we'd both want to see what's it like
being the two of us, and not ever knowing what
the other might be, but then, you know, don't you,
we're here just for a moment, and then, someday,
if we're somewhere off into the Great Beyond,
we will be everything we've ever wanted, not
knowing that we know nothing about who we are

even if we say we know so much in these few
moments finding someone like someone we'd
like to enjoy, how long, well, forever, yes,
wouldn't that be something, wouldn't that?

About the Author

DeWitt Clinton taught English, Creative Writing, and World of Ideas courses for over 30 years at the University of Wisconsin—Whitewater. Recent and past book collections include *The Conquistador Dog Texts, The Coyot. Inca Texts* (New Rivers Press), *At the End of the War* (Kelsay Books, 2018), *By A Lake Near A Moon: Fishing with the Chinese Masters* (Is A Rose Press, 2020), and *Hello There* (Word Poetry, 2021), which was awarded the 2022 Edna Meudt Poetry Book Award from the Council for Wisconsin Writers. The award also provided a short writing residency at Shake Rag Alley Center for the Arts in Mineral Point, Wisconsin. His poems and essays have appeared in a variety of national and international journals and anthologies. He is a student of Iyengar Yoga and offers a gentle but invigorating yoga class to seniors in the Milwaukee Public Library System and, occasionally, at the Village of Shorewood (Wisconsin) Senior Center.

www.ingramcontent.com/pod-product-compliance
Lightning Source LLC
Chambersburg PA
CBHW072050160426
43197CB00014B/2701